MAHATMA GANDHI

by

H. J. N. HORSBURGH

LUTTERWORTH PRESS · LONDON

22699

First published 1972

by the Lutterworth Press, Albion House,
Woking, Surrey

American edition published by the Judson Press,
Valley Forge, Pennsylvania

TO MY SON
HENGIST

ISBN **0 7188 1797 4**

COPYRIGHT © 1972 LUTTERWORTH PRESS

Printed in Great Britain
at the St Ann's Press, Park Road, Altrincham, Cheshire, WA14 5QQ

CONTENTS

INTRODUCTION

THERE IS a certain remoteness about Gandhi which has to be overcome if his relevance to the modern world is to be fully appreciated. There are several reasons for this. He has suffered the embalming process that is involved in becoming 'the father of a nation'; his severe practicality tied him to Indian conditions as he knew them, leading him to stress the spinning wheel and much else that seems far removed from the present day; he was ascetic, if not austere, and asceticism makes little appeal to contemporary Westerners; he brought his religion into all he did, and the tendency nowadays is either to discard religion altogether or to confine its influence to a small area of our lives.

Nevertheless, he connects very significantly with the modern world. His accent on natural methods and remedies links him with the work of anti-pollutionists and the present emphasis on ecology; his anti-industrial bias should be of interest to those who fear the dehumanization of contemporary society; his stress on self-reliance and the primacy of the man on the spot make him the natural ally of those who war against bureaucracy, centralization and giantism; above all, his development of a method of opposing tyranny and initiating reform without recourse to arms should recommend him to all those who combine a belief in revolutionary changes with the recognition that human inventiveness is perpetually aggravating the dangers of violence.

The present essay will centre on satyagraha the system of non-violent resistance which Gandhi developed in

South Africa and later used against the British in India and the contribution which it might make towards the solution of present-day problems.

1

LIFE

Childhood and Youth

GANDHI WAS BORN in Probandar, a seaside town in the Kathiawar Peninsula, on October 2, 1869. He belonged to the vaisya, or second lowest, Hindu caste. But his father and grandfather, both of whom were noted for their integrity, had been prime ministers of the small principality to which Gandhi belonged. So the Gandhi family was a prominent one in that locality.

Although he showed no special ability in childhood, Gandhi was expected to follow the family tradition and decided to study law as a preliminary to entering public service. He was enrolled as a student of the Inner Temple, London, in 1888 and was called to the bar in 1891. While in London he dressed as an English gentleman. But he also tended his Indian roots, mainly through the study of the Bhagavad-Gita.

On his return to India he failed as a barrister both in Rajkot and Bombay. On one occasion he lost a case through being so overcome with shyness as to be unable to speak in court. His family then obtained legal work for him from the ruling prince of Probandar. But soon afterwards, when interceding on behalf of his brother, Lakshmidas, he was rudely treated by the British Political Agent, and decided that public service in a small princi-

9

pality involved too much intrigue and sycophancy to be morally tolerable. He then accepted an invitation from the Moslem firm of Dada Abdulla & Co. to look after their legal affairs in South Africa.

Gandhi in South Africa

Gandhi landed in Durban in 1893. Except for brief intervals in India and Britain he remained in South Africa until 1914. This was the great period of his spiritual development. He entered South Africa as a shy and largely conventional Hindu lawyer; he left it as the acknowledged leader and champion of the Indian community, and as the advocate of satyagraha, a system of non-violent resistance which he had pieced together partly by trial and error and partly in creative response to the Hindu scriptures and to Thoreau, Ruskin and Tolstoy.

The turning-point in his career occurred immediately after his arrival in Durban, when, on the journey to Pretoria, he was ordered to leave his first class compartment and move to the baggage car. He refused to comply and left the train instead. Such humiliations were the common lot of Indians in South Africa. Gandhi decided that they were intolerable.

In the years that followed he gradually imbued the Indian community with a new spiritedness which enabled it to offer greater and greater resistance to the South African Government. In pursuance of this aim he successively founded two communities of resisters, first at Phoenix Farm and then at Tolstoy Farm. *Indian Opinion* was published from these centres, which were also used to train and shelter resisters and refugees. During the same period he developed his system of satyagraha.

Gandhi's struggle against the South African Government lasted eight years. It was fought over a variety of issues, notably the following: compulsory registration and finger-printing; a ban on inter-provincial immigration; taxes on former indentured labourers; and a law which denied recognition to all but Christian marriages. During the course of the struggle Gandhi first gave evidence of his capacity to stiffen opposition to authority by means of dramatic and symbolic acts of resistance. Thus, in 1908 two thousand Indians massed in a Johannesburg mosque to burn their certificates of registration; and in 1913 he defied the immigration ban by leading several thousands of Indians across the Natal border into the Transvaal. The resistance movement met with a large measure of success when the Indian Relief Act became law in July 1914.

These years of campaigning taught Gandhi a great deal about the problems and methods of non-violent resistance. He learned how hard it is to control the latent violence of resisters, and how reluctant men are to commit themselves unreservedly to the use of non-violence. He also acquired his chivalrous attitude to opponents, refusing to profit from surprise or from their temporary embarrassments. The result was that when he left South Africa he was a true satyagrahi, ready to apply his methods in the wider and more difficult context of British India.

Gandhi in India

Gandhi was slow to turn against the British. It is true that prior to his return to India in January 1915 he had written his first book, *Hind Swaraj or Indian Home Rule,* first published in 1909. But he was still prepared to cooperate with the foreign occupiers of his country, for the whole bent of his mind was towards amicable settlements and cooperation with his opponents, and also towards the minimum amount of change consistent with the attainment of justice. He did not simply want to oust the British; he wanted to liberate them from the constricting outlook of imperialism, turning them from opponents into friends. As for his own countrymen, he offered the prospect of something better than mere political independence. For *swaraj*, as Gandhi understood it, meant more than emancipation from foreign domination. It meant, not simply a change of rulers, but a change of rulers brought about by the right means, and concerning itself with freedom and equality for all. Thus, *swaraj*, in Gandhi's sense, was not sharply distinguished from *sarvodaya*, literally 'uplift for all', which was his notion of an ideal society. It follows that Gandhi was a conditional nationalist, i.e., one who promotes independence only on certain conditions. This was irksome to many of his friends and fellow countrymen, and often gave rise to sharp criticism and even to a measure of distrust.

His outlook was also responsible for apparent inconsistencies of behaviour. Thus, he has often been attacked for having recruited for the British during the first world war on the ground that this cannot be reconciled either with his faith in non-violence or with the goal of *swaraj*. But this criticism fails to take account of his distinction between the non-violence of the weak and the non-violence of the strong. Gandhi believed that non-violence is only to be preferred to violence if it is based, not on moral weakness, but on moral strength and inner conviction. In his view, such non-violence as was observable in his fellow countrymen was mainly the non-violence of the weak; and would lead them to prefer surrender to armed resistance. But for Gandhi surrender was worse than violence; and hence, in recruiting for the British he believed he was stiffening the moral fibre of his countrymen, and thereby leading them, through violence, to the higher path of non-violence. At the same time he was preparing the way for *swaraj,* a goal that had moral and not simply political implications.

Gandhi believed in long spiritual preparation for great tasks. So, on his return to India, he set up ashrams or places of religious retreat, first at Kochrab and then at Sabarmati, in the vicinity of Ahmedabad. The latter, known as Satyagraha Ashram, was his home for sixteen years. During this period he built up his immense moral authority over the Indian people, aroused the interest of Indian leaders and intellectuals in the forgotten peasantry of the subcontinent, initiated schemes for village education and sanitation, campaigned against specific injustices in many parts of the country, and led the ever-growing movement towards independence. In addition to all this he published *Young India,* and later, *Harijan,* two journals to which he himself made very frequent contributions. He also increased his immense knowledge of his country, partly through recurring tours of villages and meetings with men and women drawn from all parts and castes of India, and partly through deep immersion in every kind of problem facing his fellow countrymen. Gandhi's achievement rests squarely on his unparalleled grasp of Indian conditions and difficulties. It may be doubted whether any other modern leader has ever had as firm a grasp of his country's pulse. His eyes were open to everything, whether big or small; and it was this, as much as anything, which enabled him to choose, with so unerring an instinct, the issues which would stir the latent ardour of his people.

Within a few years of his return to India, Gandhi's influence was responsible for the use of non-violent methods of resistance on both the local and the national scale.

The first agrarian satyagraha began in 1917, in Champaran, which is in the province of Bihar. This was an indigo-growing area in which European planters and manufacturers had exploited the peasants with great ruthlessness. Eventually Gandhi was persuaded to investigate the peasants' grievances. He proceeded with the greatest thoroughness, taking statements from many thousands of villagers. Gandhi's intervention provoked the Lieutenant-Governor into setting up an official Committee of Inquiry and inviting Gandhi to participate in its activities. He agreed to do so on the condition that he was to remain the peasants' advocate. Eventually the Committee 'found in favour of the ryots, and recommended that the planters should refund a portion of the exactions made by them which the Committee had found to be unlawful. . . .'[1] But Gandhi was not content with arousing resistance to the planters' oppression. He also initiated many kinds of constructive work, e.g., village education, sanitation, and simple medical care; and such work became a regular and essential feature of every satyagraha campaign.

The struggle against the Rowlatt Bills, which led to the non-violent campaign of March-April 1919, was very different from the Champaran Satyagraha, first because it had political independence as its ultimate aim, secondly because its immediate objective was one that affected the whole country, and thirdly because it was carried on in every region of India. But violence ensued; and on April 18 Gandhi called off the campaign, claiming that it had been premature since Indians were not yet ready for non-violence. On this, as on many subsequent occasions, he showed a refreshing disposition to admit his own fallibility, freely confessing to mistakes of every kind.

These campaigns were followed by many others, some

[1] Gandhi, *My Experiment with Truth*, p. 354.

14

affecting the whole country and others—for example, the satyagraha in Bardoli[2]—being confined to a restricted area of India. For his part in the promotion of these campaigns Gandhi was sentenced in 1922 to six years' imprisonment. He was released in 1924 after an illness.

Gandhi devoted the next few years to preparing the way for the successful use of non-violence. He laid special emphasis on spinning, which he saw as a means of lessening India's economic dependence on Britain, as a symbol of self-reliance, and as a way of strengthening the will to independence. He also pleaded for friendship between Moslems and Hindus, recognizing that Indian disunity was a major cause of violence and weakness. Thus, in October 1924 he fasted against Moslem-Hindu enmity. But his efforts to heal the self-inflicted wounds of his country met with only limited success.

Gandhi's fasts were a common feature of his activity. They were intended to serve a variety of ends: the attainment of spiritual strength; the achievement of greater insight into the existing situation; the demonstration of his willingness to take upon himself the burden of suffering involved in that situation; and the proof of his concern and determination to bring about change. But they were often interpreted, both by opponents and by critical supporters, as a species of moral blackmail. They were certainly intended to convert his opponents by showing them his concern for their moral well-being. But they were also seen as coercive in character; and Gandhi did not always pay sufficient heed to the resentment to which they sometimes gave rise. It must certainly be admitted that their impact on the British stemmed from their fear lest they be held responsible for Gandhi's death rather than from any appreciation of, or response to, Gandhi's own purposes. Thus, although they some-

[2] Mahadev Desai, *The Story of Bardoli*.

times met with success, it may be doubted whether Gandhian fasting is to be recommended to advocates of non-violence. The charge of moral blackmail is a very serious one; and it must not only be undeserved but also be seen by one's opponents to be undeserved.

In 1929 Gandhi demanded independence within a year. This led to the announcement of an imperial conference and to exchanges of correspondence with Lord Irwin, the reigning viceroy. Gandhi then decided to advance the cause of emancipation by opposing the Salt Acts, which conferred a hated monopoly on the Government of India. The campaigns which followed were certainly the largest and most significant experiment in non-violence that the world has yet seen. Non-cooperation occurred on a massive scale throughout the country, and was accompanied by dramatic acts of civil disobedience. The most notable of these were a march from Ahmedabad to the coastal town of Dandi, and the attempt to take over the government salt depot at Dharasana,[3] an incident which resulted in lathi charges (in which iron-shod sticks were used against resisters) by the police and in numerous casualties. Although the Salt Acts were not repealed, they were interpreted in a more humane way, and many other concessions were made to the resisters. It was also agreed that Congress should be represented at future constitutional conferences.

Gandhi attended the Round Table Conference of 1931 as Congress's sole representative. But negotiations were fruitless, and immediately upon his return to India he was imprisoned and Emergency Powers Ordinances were proclaimed in many parts of the country. While in prison Gandhi began a fast to the death on behalf of the untouchables or harijans (literally 'children of God') as he called them. This fact (which helped to stiffen the

[3] See pp. 52–54 where I return to this incident.

16

demands of the untouchables' leader Dr. Ambedkar) led to a permanent improvement in the status of the depressed classes of India.

From 1934 to 1939 much of Gandhi's time was devoted to the promotion of spinning, basic education, language reform, dietary changes, nature cure, and other constructive activities.

Although he was not prepared to assist the British after the outbreak of war in 1939, Gandhi believed that it was the Fascist powers which were responsible for hostilities. He wanted the British to quit India and let the Indians defend themselves against the Japanese, who, by 1942, had fought their way to the frontiers of the country. He was convinced that this could be done without jeopardizing the British war effort, and threatened to mount a further civil disobedience campaign in support of independence. The British response was to imprison him and many other Congress leaders. This led to widespread violence which the viceroy, Lord Linlithgow, laid at Gandhi's door. Gandhi rejected this charge and began a three-week fast as an appeal for justice to India. He barely survived this ordeal, which failed to bring about any important change in the situation. Not long afterwards he suffered heavy personal losses through the deaths, first of his close friend and personal secretary, Mahadev Desai, and then of his wife, Kasturbai. He was released from prison in May 1944, three months after his wife's death.

In July 1945 Attlee succeeded Churchill as Britain's Prime Minister and the tempo of change began to accelerate. The great question became, not whether independence would be conceded, but whether India would be partitioned. Earlier Gandhi had tried to reach agreement with Jinnah, the Moslem leader. But his efforts came to nothing. Then, in March 1946 a British

Cabinet Mission was sent to India to discuss the country's future with Hindu and Moslem leaders. The Mission advised against partition, urging that the British Government decide in favour of a federated India with three sub-federations. Jinnah accepted this plan. Unfortunately, Gandhi was opposed to the sub-federations; and, as a consequence, Congress refused to help draft their constitutions. From that time onwards partition became more and more inevitable.

The viceroy, Lord Wavell, tried to form a provisional government representing both Congress and the Moslem League. But Jinnah refused to cooperate, except on unacceptable conditions, and announced a Direct Action Day which led to severe rioting in Calcutta. Nehru's appointment as Prime Minister on September 2 was followed by more violence. In November unsuccessful constitutional talks were held in London. Then, in February 1947, Attlee announced that Britain would relinquish control of India not later than June 1948, and that Lord Mountbatten would replace Wavell as the last viceroy of the country. Mountbatten soon concluded that partition was inescapable, and on August 15 1947 the states of India and Pakistan were established, and British rule brought to an end.

Throughout this period, and till the end of his life, Gandhi gave himself unstintingly to abating the violence which was spreading throughout the subcontinent. He visited Bengal, the Punjab and Bihar, touring for months under most taxing conditions, and trying to reconcile Hindus and Moslems. In Calcutta he fasted against communal strife, inducing Hindus, Moslems and Christians to pledge themselves to abstain from violence. These pledges were kept. He carried out a similar fast in Delhi and received further assurances from representatives of all religious faiths.

But these efforts were anathema to extreme Hindus, some of whom had formed a conspiracy to kill him. On January 30, on his way to prayers, Gandhi was assassinated.

2

SATYAGRAHA: GANDHI'S SYSTEM OF THOUGHT AND ACTION

Introduction

SATYAGRAHA IS A SYSTEM of non-violent resistance to tyranny or oppression. But it is also much more than this. Thus, at the individual level its ethical and religious roots are such as to give the satyagrahi a distinctive orientation whether he is or is not actively resisting some injustice in the community to which he belongs; and at the communal level it is a systematic attempt to make creative use of social conflict so that it becomes the means of meeting the needs of all members of the community. In brief, it is no mere collection of techniques for bringing about social changes without recourse to violence. In addition to this it is the ground plan of a distinctive and morality-pervaded way of life, both for the individual and for society at large.

Unless these wider vistas are borne in mind, the scope of satyagraha, as understood by Gandhi, cannot be adequately appreciated. And this cautionary word is the more necessary in view of the fact that, in an exposition of the present kind, the main stress inevitably falls upon the practical bearings of Gandhi's work upon the problems of the contemporary world.

The Foundations of Satyagraha

Although Gandhi never wrote a full account of his religious ideas, he did say a great deal about religion. From this it seems clear, first that he was not an unorthodox Hindu, and secondly, that his main convictions are those which seem to be central to the religious world view in its more mystical forms.

He believed that there is one God, who both transcends, and is immanent in, the universe which he has created. He also held that human beings cannot form an adequate idea of the nature of God. But we must form some idea of him; and some ideas are better than others. Thus, God is perfectly good, a God of love. Although Gandhi does not make clear why some conceptions of God are to be preferred to others, it seems probable that he saw one's idea of God as an instrument of religious experience, and believed that that conception of God is to be preferred to any other which gives us the greatest assistance in our devotional lives.

He also held that there is something akin to God in all men, however depraved; indeed, all living things have an underlying unity arising out of the relations in which they stand to God. This doctrine provides him with the religious basis of his ethical principle of *ahimsa*, something which includes but extends the Christian doctrine of the brotherhood of man. It also underlies his belief that the end of life is self-realization, where the self to be realized, since it is akin to God, can only find fulfilment in union with him. This end cannot be fully achieved in this world. But it can be pursued to an indefinite extent by seeking truth through communion with God and one's fellow men, and identifying oneself with the truth as one sees it. Thus, Gandhi's conception of self-realization is closely connected with his principle of *satya* or truth, which gave its name to his system of thought and action. It also implies acceptance of some doctrine of immortality.

The term 'satyagraha' is derived from two Sanskrit nouns, *satya,* meaning 'truth', and *agraha,* meaning 'firm-grasping'. So 'satyagraha' can be taken to mean 'holding firmly to the truth'. Thus, truth is the key conception of Gandhi's thought.

Absolute truth is identified with God. It is attained through self-realization, which, as we have seen, cannot be fully achieved in this life. It follows that in this world we must attach ourselves to the truth as we see it, i.e., to our own relative truths, where the truths in question are our beliefs about human need and the kind of society which would meet it most completely. Thus, Gandhi's quest for self-realization is the pursuit of a way of life that incorporates all the truths to which men have yet attained and which continues to strive towards Absolute Truth. This is a communal enterprise. But it is one to which each of us can bring the unique deposit of his own experiences and special opportunities. Thus Gandhi believed that human life might be so infused with truth-seeking as to become a vast 'experiment with truth'.[4]

As might be expected from what has been said, Gandhi attached the greatest importance to truthfulness. Complete openness and veracity should characterize all that one does, every effort being made to avoid the twin evils of deceiving oneself and of deceiving other people. The satyagrahi is the man who clings to truth, refusing to relinquish it either from hatred of others or from undue love of self. Simultaneously, he holds fast to what he himself believes to be the truth and does his best to do justice to the truth represented by his opponents. Thus, when he comes into conflict with others his hope is that

[4] Gandhi entitled his autobiography *My Experiments with Truth.*

truth will prevail. For he is unconditionally on the side of truth and only conditionally on the side which others take to be his own, the condition being that his side should turn out to represent truth or justice in that particular conflict.

Gandhi's second great moral principle is *ahimsa*, the literal meaning of which is harmlessness or non-injury. But this translation suggests far too negative an interpretation. *Ahimsa* is more adequately understood if it is thought of as a combination of love and of Schweitzer's 'reverence for life'. Gandhi himself described it as 'a positive state of love, of doing good even to the evil-doer'.[5] The term 'non-violence' brings out the negative side of the principle but fails to suggest the positive concern and will to service which are also essential to its meaning. In addition it obscures the religious basis of the principle which is to be found in the pervasive sense of unity generated in religious minds by the recognition of God as immanent in all that he has created.

Gandhi held that the demands of truth are absolute : in no circumstances is one justified in departing from it. But he took a rather different view of *ahimsa*, claiming that real and apparent violations of that principle were sometimes unavoidable. Apparent violations would include those cases in which a person is killed in his or her own interest. Real violations are based on systems of priorities, e.g., our recognition that the life of a snake is less valuable than that of a man. But such departures from the principle should be as few as possible and must be wholly free from the taint of malice or enmity. Even when they are unavoidable, however, they reflect upon those who have been unable to avoid them, since, had they attained to a higher moral or spiritual plane, they would have found it possible to act differently. But strict

[5] Quoted from *Young India,* January 19, 1921.

limits are placed on these concessions to human frailty. Thus, it is quite clear that the principle of *ahimsa* or non-violence must never be violated in one's dealings with one's opponents. In brief, when the satyagrahi is actively campaigning the demands of the principle of non-violence are as absolute as those of the principle of truthfulness.

Gandhi's third main principle, *tapasya,* is usually translated as 'self-suffering', meaning 'a willingness to suffer—especially on behalf of others'. It is connected with *satya* since one cannot claim to be committed to anything, let alone something as exacting as truth, unless one is prepared to suffer. It is also connected with *ahimsa* since it declares one's determination to shoulder, as far as possible, the burden of suffering which disagreements with others must often involve. Hence, *tapasya* is best seen as an implication of Gandhi's basic principles rather than as an independent moral claim. Nevertheless, it requires special mention because Gandhi believed that the satyagrahi's readiness to suffer has a vital role to play in the moral appeal which he addresses to his opponents when he decides to resist them on behalf of truth and justice.

In addition to these three principles Gandhi emphasized a number of ascetic virtues, the most important of which is *bramacharya* or sexual continence. These are seen as forms of both self-purification and self-discipline. The value of ascetic practices is now widely disputed, probably with good reason. But it cannot be doubted that the practice of satyagraha is very demanding. Hence, even if Gandhi's stress on *bramacharya* is an expression of his own unsatisfactory attitude to sex, he is right to emphasize the connections between successful non-violence and highly developed self-control. To be a true satyagrahi, firmly committed to the truth about human need, it is essential that one should be able to subjugate one's fears, envies, rages, greeds, and sexual passions.

Ends and Means in Satyagraha

Gandhi did not accept the prevailing view of the relations of ends and means—a view which involves the complete, or almost complete, subordination of means to ends. He tried to show that actions based on such a doctrine yield unsatisfactory results even from the standpoint of those who accept the doctrine. He also thought of his moral principles, and the system based upon them, as being primarily means. Hence, he can be said to have attached greater importance to means than to ends. And this conclusion is reinforced by his claim that, for the satyagrahi, means give rise to ends, not ends to means.

Gandhi insisted that 'we have always control over the means and never of the end'.[6] For him it follows that to pursue an end without reserve or limit is to be willing to commit any kind of action without ground for assurance that it is justified by one's end; and that since it is methods and not ends that one can fully control, one's responsibilities are primarily a matter of the means that one uses rather than of the ends that one either seeks or attains. He also stressed that we are liable to be mistaken, not only about what is possible, but also about the value, in relation to our ultimate objectives, of what we are trying to do. Thus, wars have often been fought to protect interests that, at the time, were described as vital, but which were soon shown to be of comparatively little importance. Again, Gandhi emphasized the organic connections between ends and means, declaring that 'there is just the same inviolable connection

[6] Quoted in B. Pattabhi Sitaramayya's *History of the Congress*, p. 979.

25

between the means and the end as there is between the seed and the tree'.[7] We reap what we sow. If our aim is to establish a society which actively seeks the fulfilment of all its members, we must restrict ourselves to the kind of means which produce such a society. We must not suppose that the brotherhood that we wish to reap will arise from seeds of hatred, falsity and treachery—the seeds that are scattered so far and wide in war and violence. To 'catch the nearest way', throwing scruples to the winds, is to ensure that one will be diverted further and further from one's ultimate goal.

The basic import of Gandhi's principles from the standpoint of the relations subsisting between means and ends can be brought out most easily by considering a number of simple imperatives. Imperatives seek to restrict action; and this is what is also involved when one makes decisions with regard either to ends or to means.

'Tell the truth' is primarily a restriction on the means we are to employ. It does not provide us with an end; and telling the truth is consistent with the choice of any end. But indirectly it is end-restrictive also, since, although it is consistent with the adoption of any end, it is a more efficient means to some ends than to others. Hence, it can be said to have a certain bias in relation to ends.

'Make people happy' is a very different kind of imperative since it provides us with an end and does not lay down any rules as to how this end is to be achieved. But it also differs markedly from an imperative such as 'Establish a system of collective security'. Three differences are specially worth noting. Making people happy is a far less determinate objective than the establishment of a system of collective security; it is far less clear how it is to be pursued because it is far less obvious, in any

[7] Gandhi, *Hind Swaraj*, p. 60.

particular case, whether it is actually being realized. Again, making people happy is an end which is continuously attainable from the time that it is first pursued, whereas the establishment of a system of collective security is an end to be achieved in the future. Finally, these imperatives differ in the degree to which they restrict our choice of means. All ends restrict one's choice of means to some extent since there is no end which can be attained by any and every course of action. But some ends are more means-restrictive than others. Establishing a collective security system is not particularly restrictive where morally significant actions are concerned. Bad faith, lying, cheating, killing, etc., are seldom efficient means to any end. But there is no reason to suppose that they are less efficient as means to the setting up of a collective security system than to an indefinitely large number of other objectives. On the other hand, there are close connections between scrupulousness and making people happy, since happiness largely depends on the quality of human relations; and these are bound to suffer if one acts unscrupulously. Again, establishing a system of collective security, in so far as it has yet to be accomplished, is an end to be attained in the future, even if it is reached in stages; and it seems to be a truth of human nature that such ends tempt us to abandon our scruples. Thus, the most ruthless men have been those who devoted themselves exclusively to ends of this kind. For any view of human society which finds its meaning in some future state of affairs in this world threatens respect for all those who oppose, or cannot contribute to, the realization of the desired end. Thus, making people happy restricts us far more in our choice of means than does the establishing of a system of collective security, partly because it imposes more stringent demands and partly because it is more inhibiting.

Gandhi's fundamental principles of *satya* and *ahimsa* are similar to the imperative 'Tell the truth' since they impose clear restrictions on our choice of means and do not provide us with any determinate objective. This entitles us to regard them as primarily means. On the other hand, they are similar to the imperative 'Make people happy' since they do lay down a general, though highly indeterminate, end. Thus, Gandhi's basic principles function partly as means and partly as ends. But their means-aspect is far more important than their end-aspect; for, considered as means, they provide us with the clearest guidance, whereas, considered as ends, their guidance is very vague indeed. And this primacy of their means-aspect is strengthened by the fact that their general objectives are of the kind which favour scrupulousness in choice of means.

Satyagraha, then, is a system of thought and action which gives pride of place to means. It retains the end-aspect of the principles on which it is founded. But it restricts us in our choice of means far more stringently than it restricts us in our choice of ends.

It provides us with the great but indeterminate objective of building a society which brings the largest measure of fulfilment to all its members. It also lays down the means whereby this objective is to be pursued. But we also require a hierarchy of more determinate ends. The selection of these cannot be arbitrary. Hence we are faced with two important questions: how do we select these ends? and how do we satisfy ourselves that we have made an acceptable selection?

In Gandhi's view, our more determinate objectives emerge from the unique combination of the existing situation and the satyagrahi's moral commitment. There are two ways in which such ends can emerge.

They often arise from one's attempt to bring one's life

into conformity with one's basic principles. This process is most easily understood by considering examples. It is obvious that certain social institutions make for violence, e.g., those which provide more opportunities for one racial group or social class than they do for others. A satyagrahi, belonging to such a community, is presented with the end of changing such institutions. But this is only a beginning. For, as he pursues this objective, he is made aware of other violence-producing institutions within his society; and gradually, as he sets himself to deal with these, he comes to frame more and more positive and comprehensive proposals for the reordering of the community—proposals which are intended not merely to sever the roots of violence but to build up a society imbued with a positive spirit of brotherhood. Thus, what begins as a simple commitment to a rule of conduct generates a hierarchy of ends which must be continuously modified and extended as further experience throws additional light on the implications, in the existing situation, of the original commitment.

Other ends emerge by a simpler process, i.e., the direct application of his principles to the existing situation. *Ahimsa* is the principle of brotherly love. Hence, wherever a need manifests itself the satyagrahi is presented with a possible determinate goal, i.e., the meeting of this need.

These processes of end-generation also test the appropriateness of the ends which are selected. For in seeking to conform with his principles in a certain situation, the satyagrahi explores, from the standpoint of his rule, the nature of his own society, growing progressively clearer about the interrelations of its institutions, and of what must be done to imbue them with his principles. It follows that, in advancing the goals which are most clearly related to his rule, he not only develops long-term objectives but can also be said to verify them. Ends are also tested in the course of every campaign, for one's opponents are confronted with the satyagrahi's relative truths about human need and challenged to correct them.

The ends which emerge from the above processes tend to become more and more comprehensive. This makes them relatively unsuitable as the aims of any specific satyagraha campaign. So the satyagrahi also needs to have immediate objectives. These are the relative truths about the existing situation with which he faces his opponents. Although these immediate aims will normally be more limited than his long-term ends, they must be very clearly connected with them. They will also provide a sharp contrast with the satyagrahi's eventual or ultimate end since they will be as markedly determinate as that is indeterminate. Hence, in an actual satyagraha campaign ends and means are both highly determinate.

Satyagraha as Making Conflict More Creative

Conflict is the most destructive force in human society. But it is also often creative, both within the individual and within society. Thus, it would be far more difficult for us to achieve tolerance and understanding of other people's weaknesses and points of view if these were not represented within ourselves, often giving rise to a measure of interior conflict. Similarly, it is largely through social conflict that different groups are made aware of one another's needs, desires and aspirations. If social conflict is ignored, or suppressed by terror, an indispensable aid to creative adjustment and development is cast aside, and conflict is bound to escalate to a level at which large-scale social disruption is highly probable or even unavoidable. Hence, civilization largely depends on our capacity, not merely to limit the destructiveness of conflict, but to make it a creative or beneficent force within human society.

Any system of non-violence is a replacement for violence. It aims to reduce the destructiveness of conflict, which now threatens to engulf our whole civilization and even to annihilate all forms of life on this planet. But it can be claimed that satyagraha goes beyond other systems of non-violence, making a still more sustained effort to wring the last drain of human advantage out of every situation involving serious disagreement. I now wish to consider the reasons which can be adduced in support of this claim, attempting to compare satyagraha both with violent methods of settling differences and also with other forms of non-violence. This should serve to bring out the distinctiveness of satyagraha considered as an answer to the problem of serious conflict.

Those whose primary commitment is to ends (whether their methods of social action be violent or non-violent) rigidly assume that their cause is just; they speak of this or the other as being 'not negotiable'. They do not see themselves, in the Gandhian fashion, as bringing about a confrontation of two sets of relative truths about human need. The justice of their cause is not something to be established; it is taken as the fixed point in their struggle with their opponents. It is true, of course, that they may feel bound to modify their demands to some extent in response to the developing situation, either because of changes in their expectations with regard to what is feasible or because of additional information on the price that is likely to be exacted for getting what they want. But these changes are seldom seen as closer approximations to the truth about human need, and their opponents are hardly ever credited with a positive role in the achievement of justice.

The Gandhian attitude to conflict is very different. The satyagrahi holds firmly to his demands while he believes them to be just. But their justice is not taken for granted or held to have been established. He remains open to rational persuasion from his opponents, and even appeals to them to confirm the moral acceptability of what he demands. Thus, the conflict between the satyagrahi and his opponents proceeds on two levels : that on which he tries to persuade them of the justice of his immediate objectives, and that on which he tries to induce them to enter into a fundamentally cooperative relationship through which the truth about relevant human needs is to be progressively unveiled and a just settlement agreed between them. Hence, although he presents a rigid surface to his opponents, refusing to make concessions which he believes to be unjust, his underlying attitude is one of flexibility, since he is urging them to cooperate with him in the achievement of a just resolution of disagreements. He does not see his opponents as mere obstacles in the path of justice ; he credits them with the capacity to make a positive contribution to a creative solution by drawing attention to relevant issues of which he is partially or wholly unaware. The surface rigidity and the underlying flexibility are two aspects of the same tireless search for truth, since one's apparent readiness to join with one's opponents in a closer study of the disputed issues would be a mere pretence if one were willing to surrender anything which one still held to be an essential requirement of justice.

It follows from what has been said that the satyagrahi should eschew the language of victory and defeat when classifying the struggles in which he has been involved. For the attainment of his immediate objectives is only sought while they are believed to be just ; if they are reached, not through a cooperative pursuit of truth but as a result of coercion, progress has not occurred at the second and more fundamental level on which the struggle is being conducted, and doubts must be cast on the moral acceptability of his objectives; and progress on the second level is hailed as a great advance even if his immediate objectives are not attained. For the aim throughout is to convert rather than to coerce one's opponents, the underlying claim being that once one has disciplined oneself to accept the verdict of human need, no matter on whose side that verdict may fall, there are no differences which cannot be overcome by negotiation, further enquiry and experiment. Coercion cannot be the satyagrahi's aim, partly because it militates against the moral development of both sides, partly because it fails to express the respect in which he holds his opponents, and partly because it does nothing to confirm the justice of his objectives.

Much of the unique creativeness of satyagraha arises out of the special features to which I have been drawing attention.

Unlike most combatants, the satyagrahi is actually seeking truth through the struggle in which he is a participant. His aim is truth, not victory. And the struggle is itself a means of attaining to the truth. For the acceptance of suffering has refining effects upon the will; and reaching the truth about questions of human need involving conflicts of interest depends very largely on surmounting wilful blindness and prejudice, i.e., upon achieving a sufficient purity of will. It is Gandhi's contention, then, that whereas some truths are reached through the systematic use of intellectual skills, other truths are attained mainly through the removal of those distortions of view which arise from the working of self-interest. Some truths are hard to discover; others are only hard to recognize or to admit. And truths about human need tend to be of the latter sort rather than of the former. Hence, the practise of satyagraha tests one's objectives more fully than any other kind of struggle; and this is essentially a creative process. Thus, satyagraha adds to the creativeness of conflict.

But much remains to be said. In particular, one must allow for the effects of a subtle interplay between the two levels on which such a struggle is being conducted. The satyagrahi's willingness to alter his objectives if they can be shown to take insufficient account of some aspect of relevant human needs reassures his opponents and also engages their respect, thereby preparing the way for a new and fundamentally cooperative relationship between the two sides. This is not only a creative process in itself, it also prepares the way for all the advances which may result from a cooperative pursuit of truth. Thus, satyagraha offers the prospect of widening the scope of human creativeness in situations of conflict to the point at which all those involved in a dispute are making a positive contribution to its resolution. As much can be said for no other system of social action, whether that system be violent or non-violent in character.

Nor is this all, for it omits a whole dimension of satyagraha, namely, that of constructive work. Gandhi insisted that resisting injustice never exhausts the moral requirements of any situation. Indeed, he went further and claimed that resistance, even by non-violent means, is morally unjustifiable unless it is accompanied by some attempt to make constructive use of the situation. It is probable that his main reason for taking this view was serious doubt with respect to the constructive intentions of those whose efforts can ever be confined to resisting the policies and intentions of others. He believed that the basic values of satyagraha should be able to find expression, not merely in non-violent resistance, but also in some directly creative response to the developing situation. Other practical moral reasons why he emphasized constructive work almost certainly included the following : the need to maintain a constant awareness of one's basic concerns and the wider contexts of one's actions; the importance of providing one's opponents with evidence of one's constructive intentions; and the necessity of maintaining a very high level of discipline among the non-violent resisters themselves. All these purposes are served by constructive work. It counteracts the tendency of conflict to narrow down one's interest till it is focused exclusively on the struggle itself, bringing about a serious loss of sense of proportion. Again, opponents who combine resistance with self-reliant schemes of reform are likely to elicit an increasingly favourable response. Also, the latent violence of less disciplined resisters is curbed by being given constructive tasks to perform. But the most vital feature of constructive work is that it injects a stream of creative activities into the very heart of potentially destructive situations, revealing in an absolutely unambiguous way the positive thrust of satyagraha towards the fulfilment of human need. The satyagraha struggle attempts to test one's relative truths and to win the cooperation of one's opponents; it is an indirect contribution to the meeting of human need. But constructive work aims at a direct contribution. It is the expression of a belief that creative goodwill should never be held up, awaiting the outcome of some struggle in which it may be engaged; in addition to pressing on with resistance in an indirectly creative way, it should also be seeking some avenue of direct service to those who are involved in that struggle.

For all these reasons, then, it can be contended that satyagraha adds enormously to the creativeness of conflict. It does so, first by turning disagreement into an instrument for the attainment of truth, and secondly by refusing to allow any dispute to hold up the deployment of truth in the service of those whose interests are affected by the conflict.

All this is germane to the effectiveness of the moral appeal to one's opponents which lies at the heart of satyagraha. Gandhi believed that nobody is so corrupt as to lie entirely out of reach of such appeals, especially if one's good will is made sufficiently manifest and one's willingness to suffer for the truth is clearly demonstrated. There can be no certainty that one's opponents will respond to this moral appeal : if a response were certain the appeal would have ceased to be moral in character. But one's evident attachment to the truth, one's readiness to suffer, and one's resistance (which takes forms that cannot be ignored) combine to create a situation in which everything possible is done to bring about the conversion of one's opponents.

Preparations for Satyagraha

The phrase 'preparations for satyagraha' can be used with different degrees of inclusiveness. It can be confined to preparations for a specific campaign; it can be broadened to include preparations for a whole series of campaigns aiming at a fairly distant or long-term objective, i.e., *swaraj* in India; and it can be widened still further to take in the cultivation, over a long period of time, of those qualities without which one cannot hope to function as an effective satyagrahi.

All these different sorts of preparations are important. But those which aim at character development and heightened discipline deserve pride of place, for the effectiveness of satyagraha depends primarily upon the moral quality and self-control of those by whom it is used. Intellectual skills, especially those of an intuitive kind, are important to its success, but, in the absence of that moral force which has distinguished all the great exponents of non-violence, such skills are of little value.

What are the qualities on which Gandhi placed the greatest emphasis? In addition to those underlined by his basic principles, such as truthfulness and loving concern for others, the qualities which he most valued are fearlessness, patience, self-reliance and freedom from covetousness.

It is hardly necessary to say anything of truthfulness and loving concern for others, for if these qualities are absent one cannot claim to be a satyagrahi at all. Truthfulness is essential if one is to hold steadfastly to truth; and *ahimsa* is reduced to mere harmlessness unless it is sustained by a loving concern for one's fellows.

Gandhi's emphasis on fearlessness (which he equates with courage) has its source in his basic principles as well as in the demands of non-violent social action. He saw it as an aspect of attachment to truth. The coward, in Gandhi's view, is the man who shrinks from reality, refusing either to understand or to deal with the truths that are relevant to his situation. But fearlessness is also needed if one is to renounce the use of violence and yet continue to resist those who have the power to kill or injure. Such fearlessness is essential if one's non-violence is to be the non-violence of the strong, i.e., the non-violence of conviction and not of mere expediency. The non-violence of the weak is the non-violence of those who lack the courage to be violent; the non-violence of the strong is the non-violence of those who have that special courage which enables one to confront injustice without the aid of physical weapons.

Timidity undermines one's will to resist; impatience erodes one's will to resist non-violently. Hence, satyagraha is impossible unless one achieves a high level of patience. It has also to be remembered that a moral appeal to one's opponents forms the core of Gandhi's method. One cannot hope to convert one's opponents by means of such an appeal unless one has the patience to await a favourable response without backsliding into violence.

Gandhi also emphasizes self-reliance. This is because habitual self-reliance makes for fearlessness just as dependence on others tends to generate anxiety. But it is mainly due to its direct and vital bearing on the practise of satyagraha. There are many reasons for its importance, most of them connected with the decentralized manner in which non-violent pressures tend to be applied. But a further reason lies in the fact that satyagrahi leaders are necessarily left at the mercy of one's opponents who may imprison or execute them at the start of a non-violent campaign. It is essential, therefore, that qualities of self-reliance should be developed far down the hierarchy of resisters.

Finally, Gandhi stressed freedom from covetousness on the grounds that an acquisitive state of mind makes for anxiety, fearfulness and violence. Also, greedy men are for sale. It follows that acquisitiveness presents one's opponents with the means of sapping the strength of a resistance movement by effecting its partial corruption.

It is clear that, in Gandhi's view, these qualities are produced most effectively by a highly developed religious life. He repeatedly stresses the need for daily prayer and meditation, claiming that they not only develop the qualities which are most vital to non-violent action but that in times of special difficulty they reinforce and purify the will. As we have already seen, Gandhi's practice of fasting at times of crisis also has a religious basis. His use of the ashram or religious retreat, further underlines the special place which he gives to religious practices in his system of training. Such ashrams were used by him for many purposes: as places where one could attain by meditation to deeper insight into the existing situation; for the training of satyagrahi leaders; as centres from which to organize constructive work, and as campaign headquarters. Again, he explicitly connects fearlessness and belief in God. 'A non-violent man can do nothing save by the power and grace of God. Without it he won't have the courage to die without anger, without fear, and without retaliation. Such courage comes from the belief that God sits in the hearts of all, and that there should be no fear in the presence of God.'[8]

The next most effective means of developing character is service to one's fellow men. Thus, Gandhi also emphasizes constructive work in this connection.

A whole lifetime is not too long in which to prepare oneself for satyagraha. The qualities on which it depends come slowly if they come at all. But there is also a place for more intensive methods of training, which aim, not at fundamental changes of character, but at the attainment of a high level of discipline. In recent years such methods have been used by anti-racist groups in the U.S.A. They were also used in India. Thus, Gandhi gave his blessing to the formation of several organizations which drilled and disciplined their members in a quasi-military fashion.[9] Organizations of this kind are potentially vital since effective non-violence depends upon the achievement of specially high levels of social discipline.

[8] Gandhi, *Non-violence in Peace and War*, vol. 1, p. 145.
[9] Quami Seva Dal and the Khudai Khidmatgars.

Other methods of raising discipline which were used by Gandhi include the following: propaganda, constructive work, limited satyagraha campaigns, and the taking of oaths and pledges. Discipline is reinforced if a community is made aware of the precise issues involved in a struggle and of how much depends on the avoidance of violence. Constructive work is equally valuable since it raises satyagrahis to positions of leadership in local affairs, enabling them to gain the trust and regard of the local community so that it is prepared to remain non-violent even in situations of danger and high provocation. It also brings them greater knowledge of local affairs. This knowledge serves many purposes, including that of helping them to control communal weaknesses and conflicts. Limited satyagraha campaigns[10] give valuable training in the use of non-violent methods and the maintenance of discipline in hazardous and upsetting situations. They also serve one of the same functions as constructive work: that of giving expression to militancy that might otherwise lead to violence. Furthermore, in so far as they remove injustices they reinforce popular belief in satyagrahi leaders and in their techniques. Finally, Gandhi's use of the pledge did much to ensure social discipline and to bring home to ordinary men and women what they would be expected to do in all the different kinds of situations which were most likely to arise. Thus immediately prior to the Independence Campaign of 1930–31 Gandhi published in *Young India* a set of rules which was to be strictly observed by all resisters in the ensuing campaign. Large numbers of Indians pledged themselves to adhere to these rules.

I pass now to Gandhi's methods of organizing resistance, a subject on which I shall confine myself to

[10] E.g., the Vykom Temple Road Satyagraha. See Joan Bondurant, *Conquest of Violence,* pp. 46–52.

matters on which his views seem to be of lasting value to those engaged in satyagraha campaigning.

The first of these relates to the structure of non-violent resistance organizations and arises out of two of the satyagrahi's most essential characteristics: knowledge of his own locality and self-reliance. Gandhi believed that wherever possible non-violent resistance should be left in the hands of local leaders. It is better to remove an injustice from one's own shoulders than to have it removed by other people; nothing is more local and particular than human need, and hence, if one proposes to alleviate suffering, one should act under orders from those who have the most far-reaching knowledge of local affairs; unnecessary provocation should not be given to opponents, and there is something singularly offensive in the idea of a group of travelling revolutionaries wandering round a country stirring up resentment. The activities of such a group tend to be self-defeating since it is easy for one's opponents to question the seriousness of injustices which do not appear to be felt till attention is drawn to them by itinerant trouble-makers.

All this tells in favour of a cellular type of organization. And there are other considerations which confirm this inclination: the special vulnerability of leaders in a non-violent movement, and the need to attain to that degree of economic self-reliance which will enable one to continue resistance under conditions that would force the collapse of any movement which is centrally organized and controlled.

In Gandhi's view, resistance is mobilized mainly through propaganda and constructive work. Much of Gandhi's propaganda was purely factual in character, its intention being to inform both Indians and Britons of the realities of the existing situation. In this he was much assisted by the strong local roots of his movement which could be used both to gather information and to publicize it. Making people aware of the facts and urging them to resist are only the first steps in propaganda, however. They must be followed or accompanied by demonstrations of various kinds, the most important of which will be those which highlight particular injustices and prepare the way for satyagraha campaigning. Minor campaigns are also an effective form of propaganda, since they can do a great deal to build resistance and to foster popular confidence in satyagrahi leaders and non-violent methods.

Constructive work has a vital place in promoting resistance. In addition to turning satyagrahis into trusted leaders it results in improved conditions, and such improvements are usually accompanied by lessening apathy and a greater willingness to accept the risks which open resistance must involve. Constructive work is also an earnest of the satyagrahi's good will. Hence, it can do much to bring about that change of heart in one's opponents which is the central aim of all Gandhian resistance.

It is now necessary to say something about the selection of immediate objectives, i.e., about the goals of specific satyagraha campaigns. First, these objectives should be highly determinate. This tends to reassure one's opponents since demands are often vaguely expressed in order to conceal one's true aims. Secondly, they should be clearly related to one's preparations for the campaign. For example, although part of one's propaganda activity may look forward towards long-term ends it should be concentrated mainly on the realization of one's specific goals. Thirdly, they should include the remedy or prevention of some serious injustice. Unless this is the case one cannot direct a clear moral challenge towards one's opponents. Furthermore, the seriousness of the injustice should be such as to warrant the social disorganization which must ensue. Fourthly, wherever possible they should favour dramatic methods of campaigning. Such methods intensify interest and stiffen popular resistance. Fifthly, they should point forward as clearly as possible towards the more comprehensive or long-term ends of the resistance movement. Finally, they should open up the prospect of fruitful negotiation with one's opponents. This will be much easier to do in some conflicts than in others. What is particularly vital is that one's opponents should be safeguarded from humiliation. All these requirements are closely connected with the essential nature of satyagraha, namely, that it is a moral appeal directed at one's opponents.

These objectives are negotiable in the sense that one's opponents are challenged to show that they take inadequate account of some aspect of the situation. But it must be clear that the satyagrahi's demands cannot be amended until good reasons have been provided for altering them, and that, since the issues are serious ones, active resistance will commence at such and such a time unless acceptable proposals are received at an earlier date. Thus, the satyagrahi's preparations culminate in an ultimatum which will disclose to his opponents his plans for resistance and also the exact date on which active resistance will begin.

Satyagraha in Action

Gandhi's teaching on satyagraha in action can be presented under the following divisions: the general rules to be followed when campaigning, the principal methods of resistance, and the different stages through which a large-scale campaign may be expected to pass if it runs its full course.

All the rules of campaigning with which I shall deal are concerned, directly or indirectly, with preserving or improving the moral quality of the satyagrahi, or with ensuring that his opponents do not evade the moral challenge which he addresses to them.

It follows that many of the satyagrahi's preparations for a non-violent conflict should be continued throughout the ensuing campaign. This is specially true of all forms of self-development, whether moral or religious in character. These are vital in themselves, and also as evidence of the satyagrahi's sincerity and of his wish to enter into cooperative relationships with his opponents even while active resistance is taking place. For satyagraha is quite different from warfare. In warfare, military leaders set their faces against fraternization, let alone cooperation, with the enemy; in satyagraha, contact with opponents is actively sought and any form of cooperation that is not at odds with the objectives of the campaign is positively encouraged by the satyagrahi leadership. Ignorance of others is the breeding ground of suspicion and distrust. Hence, satyagrahis want to make themselves known as thoroughly as possible to their opponents.

Constant self-examination is also essential. Some resisters may have personal failings to overcome; parts of the resistance movement may be showing signs of diminishing morale; other groups of resisters may be displaying a militancy that might discharge itself in violence; conflicts may be developing between different groups of resisters. All these deficiencies have to be pinpointed and actively combated at the earliest opportunity. This is vital if one is engaged in warfare; it is still more vital if one is involved in a non-violent struggle, partly because one's aim is to present a moral challenge, and partly because a satyagraha movement cannot protect itself as easily from the fragility of its weakest members as can a terrorist conspiracy or a nation at war. Believers in violence can simply eliminate traitors and defectors; satyagrahis have to use more humane and subtle methods.

In spite of the best efforts of satyagrahi leaders, control of the movement may be lost, either because resistance collapses or because enthusiasm brims over into violence. If the morale of resisters fails it is plain that preparations have been inadequate. In such circumstances active campaigning has to be ended and fresh efforts made to arouse and organize opposition to one's opponents. Serious outbreaks of violence may also necessitate the suspension of a campaign. Gandhi's practice varied in the face of large-scale indiscipline. Sometimes he suspended a campaign altogether; sometimes he allowed it to continue on a diminished scale; sometimes he proceeded with his original plans. What seems to be clear is that, when violence occurs on any considerable scale, control over the movement must take priority over active resistance.

Efforts must also be made to retain the initiative since situations of stalemate and apparent inactivity tend to sap morale. The more dramatic forms of campaigning are important in this connection. But constructive work is still more vital, first because it sets a movement to work, and secondly because it offers progress in some desired direction to compensate for any lack of progress towards the immediate objectives of the campaign.

Most of the techniques of non-violence are well-known in the west. Thus, the strike, the boycott and social ostracism have all been used in industrial disputes, and civil disobedience and non-cooperation have been

45

employed by groups of war resisters in many different countries. But a large variety of such methods have been used in India, and some of these have not acquired special names in the west.

The techniques of non-cooperation deserve special emphasis since they must form the backbone of resistance in any large-scale struggle aiming at fundamental changes. Many such methods were used in India, some far more important than others. The hard core of resisters surrendered or rejected honours, titles and honorary offices, refused to lend money to the government, and boycotted British goods. These forms of non-cooperation were employed continuously over a long period. Other methods came into use during times of more active resistance, e.g., the boycotting of law courts, schools, colleges and legislative councils, withdrawal from all forms of government service (including the police and armed forces), the refusal to use or to provide banking and insurance services, withholding labour by closing shops and other businesses, and the organization of *hizrat,* which involves withdrawal from an area where a certain injustice is taking place.

It may seem contradictory that believers in cooperation should resort to such methods. The answer is that the satyagrahi is prepared to cooperate with anyone provided that the enterprise is consistent with his own objectives and the principles from which they have emerged. But sometimes the basic situation leaves little room for cooperation.

Non-cooperation, if it is carried far enough and is organized on a sufficiently massive scale, can ensure the overthrow of any system of central authority. But this is only possible if the movement of resistance is both large and highly disciplined. Hence, such a movement often requires to take action against the apathy or defection of its own potential supporters. In India, for example, the less spirited and reliable members of the community were sometimes opposed by such methods as picketing, the sit-down strike and social ostracism. These methods seriously exercised Gandhi's conscience. Thus, he refused to countenance *dhurna* or the sit-down strike as an aid to picketing, mainly because he felt that it involved intimidation and moral blackmail. But he seems to have thought that it was permissible when used against hardened aggressors. He was also reluctant to resort to social ostracism but appears to have thought that it was sometimes unavoidable as a method of social discipline.

Civil disobedience can take as many forms as non-cooperation : indeed many methods of resistance (e.g., the refusal to pay taxes) can be regarded as methods of both non-cooperation and civil disobedience. Some forms of civil disobedience have the same long-term cumulative effects as methods of non-cooperation; others are more spectacular and aim with greater precision at particular effects. The effectiveness of some forms of civil disobedience depends upon the active support of large numbers of people; others can be used successfully by a handful of courageous and devoted men and women.

Obviously the stages through which a satyagraha campaign can be expected to pass depend on the general situation in which non-violent resistance is being offered. If the aim is to remove a specific injustice in a particular area of a country, there is no regular sequence of stages. The oppressors may decide to relent; on the other hand, they may bear down still more heavily upon resisters. Cases will differ endlessly. But if an oppressed population is offering satyagraha with a view to its political emancipation, and the methods of non-cooperation and civil

47

disobedience are applied wholeheartedly against all the institutions of oppression, the machinery of political and social life will be progressively paralysed. In such circumstances the campaign may move on to a stage which has been called assertive satyagraha.[11] This stage has been reached when central control has been largely wrested from one's opponents and some of the functions of government are exercised by resistance leaders. It culminates in the complete usurpation of central authority and the establishment of parallel government. The beginnings of this stage were reached in India on a number of occasions. For example, the Bombay Congress Committee instituted a system of taxation for those who accepted its authority, and in many places a programme of national education was worked out and partially developed. These experiments were terminated by the Gandhi-Irwin Pact of March 5, 1931. Later experiences of a similar kind led to widespread violence and suggest that the control of a non-violent resistance movement may be especially difficult when the assertive stages of the campaign have been reached.

Illustrations

The literature of non-violent case histories is now considerable. Even that part of the literature which is confined to Indian experience runs to many volumes. Non-violent methods have been used with partial or complete success in many different parts of the world (e.g., South Africa, India, the U.S.A., Norway, Denmark, Hungary, etc.) and they have been used effectively against extremely tough and brutal opponents (e.g., the Nazis in Norway during the second world war).[12] In

[11] By Krishnalal Shridharani. See his *War without Violence*.

[12] See Gene Sharp, *Tyranny Could Not Quell Them!* Published by *Peace News* in 1959.

what follows I do not propose to describe any complete case history. Instead, I shall confine myself to illustrating a few special features of satyagraha which either deserve greater emphasis or which may be more adequately understood once they have been illustrated.

It is particularly important to give examples of constructive work. Gandhi once called it 'the permanent part of non-violent effort',[13] and emphasized it ceaselessly in his articles and speeches. Yet it is apt to seem little more than a vague penumbra of resistance until it is sharpened and clarified by actual cases. In the final section of this essay I hope to show that it is one of Gandhi's great legacies to the world, and that its neglect has been the principal reason why non-violent methods have often failed.

Even in his earliest campaigns in South Africa, Gandhi promoted activities concerned with 'internal improvement'. These were the forerunners of constructive work. As an aspect of his method it is almost fully developed by the time he organized the first agrarian satyagraha in Champaran, which I have already referred to in my outline of his career. I shall now return to this satyagraha.

After Gandhi had been working in the area of Champaran for some time he saw that no permanent improvement in the condition of the peasants was possible unless a constructive programme was instituted. He decided to open primary schools in six villages. But he was not able to find local teachers who were prepared to do this work for 'a bare allowance or without remuneration'. So teachers were brought in from other parts of India. Through these schools influence was exerted not only on the children themselves but also on the village women. Skin diseases and other ailments were

[13] *Harijan,* May 18, 1940.

extremely common because of the filthy conditions in which people lived. So primary education was combined with the promotion of sanitation and the provision of simple medical relief. The Servants of India Society was approached and a doctor found to organize this important work. At first the villagers were not prepared to do anything for themselves. But by degrees, after roads had been swept, wells cleared, and pools filled up by volunteers, many of them began to cooperate with their unpaid helpers.

As a consequence of all this work the satyagrahis gained the confidence and respect of the village communities and were able to influence their behaviour in such a way as to bring about lasting changes.[14]

One further point is to be noted in connection with this constructive programme: those who took part in it were expressly charged not to concern themselves with politics or with grievances against the planters. Those making complaints were to be referred to Gandhi. 'No one was to venture out of his beat.' The moral here is that although constructive work is a regular preparation for, and accompaniment of, satyagraha, it should be disentangled from resistance and carried on as a largely independent activity even though those taking part in it may also have a role in active campaigning. The value of this separation lies in the way it underlines the fact that constructive work is not being promoted simply as an aspect of a campaign; it looks beyond present injustices to a future in which self-reliant action will create an improved form of society. Hence, there is nothing artificial about constructive work. It is not tacked on to resistance as a largely optional extra. If

[14] For Gandhi's own account of this campaign, see *Experiments with Truth,* pp. 337–354. See also Rajendra-Prasad's *Satyagraha in Champaran.*

those who are engaged in it are true satyagrahis it will be proceeded with, in season and out, regardless of whether active resistance is or is not in progress. Thus it would be truer to say that resistance is tacked on to constructive work than to say that constructive work is tacked on to resistance.

I now wish to illustrate the value of a minor, and not particularly successful, satyagraha, as a means of building up spiritedness and resistance, thereby preparing the way for more important and large-scale campaigning.

The aim of the Kheda Satyagraha[15] was to bring relief to the peasants of the Kheda district in the Gujarat who had been reduced to the verge of famine by the failure of their crops. The Land Revenue Rules under which they operated provided for a total remission of assessments if crop yields fell below one quarter of their normal level. Gandhi and his helpers carried out an enquiry which showed that land dues should be remitted. But government officials contested this and refused to accept the peasants' petitions on the ground that they had been improperly submitted.

When the Governor of Bombay refused to take any action Gandhi advised the peasants to resort to satyagraha. A pledge was drawn up and signed by the resisters. Its signatories undertook not to pay their dues even if this resulted in the loss of their land. As the peasants went in dread of having their land confiscated it was no easy matter to bring them to the point of signing such a pledge. Nevertheless, Gandhi and his followers succeeded in reassuring them to such a degree that they not only overcame their fear of officials but stood in danger of needlessly antagonizing them. Consequently, Gandhi had to urge them to combine fearless-

[15] See Gandhi's own account, *Experiments with Truth,* pp. 362–367.

ness with courtesy. Civility, he writes, 'is the most difficult part of satyagraha. Civility does not . . . mean the mere outward gentleness of speech . . . but an inborn gentleness and desire to do the opponent good. These should show themselves in every act of a satyagrahi'.[16]

Although initially the government reacted with severity, and many peasants suffered hardship, concessions were eventually made to the poorer peasants, and Gandhi decided that these were sufficient to justify him in calling off the campaign. In spite of the fact that the Kheda Satyagraha did not fully achieve its objectives it was most valuable because it marked 'the beginning of an awakening among the peasants of the Gujarat, the beginning of their true political education. . . .'

An additional example of civil disobedience may also be valuable to those who are unfamiliar with the literature of non-violence. I shall therefore say more about the Salt Acts Satyagraha mentioned earlier.

Preparations for this campaign were very thorough. Training was provided for volunteers, those taking part in the first action were carefully selected, and nobody was allowed to participate in any action without first pledging himself to non-violence and obedience. These preparations culminated in an ultimatum from Gandhi to the viceroy, Lord Irwin.

The campaign began with a march of 200 miles from Ahmedabad to Dandi, on the coast. On reaching the sea the satyagrahis extracted salt from the sea-water, thereby infringing the letter of the Salt Acts. This set off a nation-wide wave of civil disobedience, its size being such as to astonish the more westernized and sceptical of Indian leaders.

In May 1930 Gandhi again wrote to Lord Irwin informing him of the satyagrahis' intention of taking

[16] Gandhi, *Experiments with Truth*, p. 364.

over the large government salt depot at Dharasana. Gandhi was arrested prior to the raid. But the satyagrahis went ahead with their plans. Almost at once they were attacked by police armed with lathis. The satyagrahis refused to defend themselves and large numbers were injured. The government attempted to suppress news of these lathi charges. But many eye-witness accounts are available, including some from well-known American journalists, such as Webb Miller and Negley Farson. The following is part of Miller's account: 'Suddenly, at a word of command, scores of native policemen rushed upon the marchers, and rained blows on their heads with steel-shod lathis. Not one of the marchers even raised an arm to fend off the blows. . . . In two or three minutes the ground was quilted with bodies. Great patches of blood widened on their white clothes. The survivors without breaking ranks silently and doggedly marched on until struck down. . . .'[17]

With the coming of the monsoon, which makes the open-air evaporation of sea-water impossible, the raids on salt depots were ended. But resistance continued in other ways: foreign goods were boycotted, shops which ignored the boycott were picketed, and the special ordinances introduced by the government against the satyagrahis were disobeyed. The use of these forms of resistance only stopped after the Gandhi-Irwin Agreement of March 5, 1931.

The Salt Acts were not repealed. But they were reinterpreted in such a way as to make them less of a hardship to poorer Indians. The special ordinances were also withdrawn, pardons were granted to those guilty of civil disobedience, and confiscated property was returned to its original owners.

The interest of the Salt Acts Satyagraha stems from

[17] Quoted from Roy Walker, *Sword of Gold*, pp. 111-112.

the facts that it was organized on the largest scale, that the satyagrahis continued to resist non-violently in the face of wholesale police brutality, and that methods were used which stimulated the imagination and strengthened the resistance of the Indian masses. The campaign is also of importance because of the efforts which were made to prevent outbreaks of violence. In addition to insisting on the taking of a pledge, Gandhi tried to restrict the more active campaigning to those parts of the country which had been most fully prepared, and also warned his followers that if they broke their word satyagraha would be used against them. In later years he used this method repeatedly to oppose Hindu-Moslem strife.

3

GANDHI'S CONTRIBUTION

INJUSTICES ABOUND in the contemporary world. Count-less millions have insufficient to eat while millions more grow fat through excessive eating. Whole classes and racial groups are condemned to a stultifying exist-ence. Gross neglect is commonly the lot of the sick, the poor, the educationally underprivileged, and the old, even in those communities which pride themselves on having established the welfare state. So vast changes are essential. Some of these can be brought about by con-stitutional means. But there are many countries where intolerable conditions cannot be wholly remedied if one restricts oneself to those methods which have the approval of law. In the Union of South Africa, for example, there is no serious prospect of fully lifting the hand of racial oppression by legally permissible means. Yet modern science and technology have escalated the effects of violence to a point at which all but the most insensitive must shrink from its unrestricted use to bring about social change. In such circumstances it is not surprising that large numbers of men and women have developed an interest in non-violent direct action.

But it is very difficult to persuade people to commit themselves unreservedly to non-violence. This is due to many factors, including the following: (i) our educational systems still subtly implant a belief in the effectiveness of violence, e.g., through the way in which history is customarily taught; (ii) human impatience releases a militancy which is difficult to control, and popular impatience is increasing rather than diminishing; and (iii) conflict tends to generate hatred, and hatred readily leads to a denial of the possibility of converting one's opponents as well as to a tendency to exaggerate their powers. This produces a drive towards extreme methods, effectively undermining the scruples which stand between resisters and the most savage forms of violence.

All these factors have not only discouraged the use of non-violence but have also militated against its success. For non-violence is very demanding. Physical force is probably used most effectively by those who use it with extreme reluctance; such effectiveness as it has in no way depends upon a disbelief in the usefulness of other methods of social action. But non-violence cannot hope to have any great effectiveness in the absence of an all-out commitment to its use, partly because it depends on a degree of discipline that is most unlikely to be maintained if one is continuously debating whether to revert to the use of violence, and partly because it contains a moral appeal, the genuineness of which is necessarily undermined by doubts and hesitations as to whether violence is to be preferred. The non-violence of anti-racist movements in South Africa and the U.S.A. appears to have been mainly the non-violence of expediency. It has not sprung from any great depth of conviction. Hence, when it has met with apparent lack of success, disillusionment has spread rapidly among most of its users, who have quickly reverted to violence. But is this inevitable?

Deep attachment to non-violent methods and values is something which cannot be expected to develop rapidly in ordinary men and women. The problem, therefore, is that of finding some method of building up faith in non-violence to the point at which its potential as a beneficent force in our civilization has a serious chance of being realized. How is this to be done?

In my view, the trend to violence could be reversed if Gandhi's teaching on constructive work were seriously heeded. For constructive work has the power to counter the factors that make for belief in violence. It is all the more to be regretted, therefore, that this side of Gandhi's method has been disregarded. Thus, in recent years non-violent methods of resistance have been used in many parts of the world (e.g., the Union of South Africa, the U.S.A., Norway, Britain, Czechoslovakia, etc.) sometimes by men and women who have believed themselves to be applying Gandhi's methods; but in no case, so far as I am aware, has any attention been given to this vital aspect of satyagraha. Martin Luther King, for example, was an avowed follower of Gandhi. But if one turns to his account of the non-violent campaign which he led in Montgomery, Alabama, one finds no mention of constructive work; and it is only too likely that this neglect is at least partly responsible for the resurgence of violence in the anti-racist movement of the U.S.A.[18]

I shall now say something about the bearing of constructive work on each of the factors mentioned above, especially (ii) and (iii).

Popular impatience is a problem that is being steadily aggravated by several features of the contemporary world. This is partly due to the decline in religious belief. For, as religion loses its hold, death acquires a finality that drives men to speed the processes of change. Again, our expectations have been increased by the rapidity of technological development. We are the victims of a false analogy. We fail to notice that the social changes that we

[18] See his book, *Stride Towards Freedom*. Nevertheless, this is a profoundly moving book.

57

wish to bring about are more like processes of education than like progress in science or industry; and formal education extends over a longer period today than ever before. The fundamental but often subtle adjustments which are needed in most present-day communities cannot be satisfactorily undertaken in a short period of time. To rush to the barricades in an effort to achieve an instant transformation of society is either to worsen tyranny or to replace one form of oppression with another. Lasting improvements are like processes of maturation and cannot be carried out at high speed. Another factor is that science has produced an experimental mentality which makes us reluctant to persist in courses that do not meet with rapid success; and non-violent methods are often slow, and also depend for their effectiveness on a firm commitment on the part of their users. They are a species of social therapy; and the body politic takes time to heal. Only those who have a well-grounded faith in non-violence are prepared to forgo the surgery of violence. Finally, there seems to be something undemocratic and morally objectionable about the use of methods which do not promise quick results. For the slower one's methods the longer it must take before large companies of people enjoy their proper share of the community's wealth and attention. But this is a serious snare if sureness demands slowness.

Gandhian constructive work offers an answer to the problem of mass impatience. To begin with, it provides worth-while occupation for a movement's popular support. It also maintains morale by ensuring some kind and degree of progress. This is able to compensate for apparent lack of headway towards the specific objectives of the struggle. Finally, it offers additional fields in which devoted volunteers can give lessons in non-violent action, thereby deepening popular understanding of satyagraha. It scarcely needs to be said that this is not an easy answer. Much care and skill is required to work out an effective constructive programme, especially if it is to absorb the energies of large numbers of resisters. But it is highly questionable whether the violence of growing impatience can be curbed by any other means.

Constructive work also combats hatred and that sense of impotence which gives such powerful reinforcement to feelings of enmity. It does so in a variety of ways. First, it maintains a real awareness of one's fundamental aims and the wider vistas opened up by one's actions. The effect of this is to neutralize the tendency of conflict to lead to a miserable constriction of interest which progressively blinds one to everything except the day-to-day detail of the struggle in which one is engaged. Non-violent resistance, when properly combined with constructive work, actively supports and confirms one's long-term ends, keeping one in a state of recollection. In the fullest sense, one remembers who one is, what one is setting out to do, and its importance as seen in the light of one's most far-reaching goals. Secondly, constructive work forces one to recall, what violence encourages one to forget, that the power of one's opponents is limited. There may be many valuable enterprises which they are in a position to frustrate. But no imaginable tyranny can call a complete halt to all the creative interactions between the existing situation and the basic principles of Gandhism.

All this can be illustrated by reference to Gandhi's own objective of political independence. Although political emancipation is of the greatest importance, it is neither everything in itself nor is it an essential presupposition of all that one is trying to achieve. So Gandhi displaces the mistaken belief that political freedom or equality must be realized before any other kind of freedom or equality can be exercised. He raises the questions: why are you seeking political independence? And is it not the case that much of what you want can be realized by your unaided efforts before independence is achieved? The effect of such questions is simultaneously to restore one's sense of proportion and to sever the roots of one's pervasive sense of impotence. Thus, he states the fundamentals of his view shortly and unmistakably at the beginning of *Constructive Programme: Its Meaning and Place* where he insists that 'the constructive programme is the truthful and non-violent way of winning *Poorna Swaraj*. Its wholesale fulfilment IS complete independence.'

In my view, all this is immediately applicable to the situation of the American Negro and even of the Russian-dominated Czech. He lies under a yoke, but that yoke does not reduce him to complete helplessness. His efforts do not need to be confined to the removal of that yoke. Much that he aims to do with the freedom for which he is struggling can be done, here and now, while he is still fighting to win that freedom.

Consider water building up behind a dam. The water does not allow its progress to be checked by the dam if there is some other direction in which it can advance in conformity with the laws of gravity. So it is with the satyagrahi who resorts to constructive work. Resistance does not monopolize his attention. He does not remain in a state of frustration until he can spill over the dam raised by his opponent's opposition. He is fluid and alive to all the creative possibilities of the situation, ready to advance in any direction just so long as it is in conformity with the basic principles of satyagraha. The only difference that we need to notice between the two cases is that water is sometimes contained on every side, whereas no group of human beings can ever be confined to the same degree. Human creativity can always find a channel if it is sufficiently determined to do so.

Finally, constructive work can be said to counter belief in the special effectiveness of violence. This follows straighforwardly from what has already been said. Constructive work shows us what can be accomplished by non-violent means; and simultaneously, makes clear to us what cannot be prevented by any imaginable degree of violence. Hence, the human creativity which expresses itself in constructive work is the best possible argument against the unique effectiveness of violence.

Enough has been said, I think, to show that Gandhi's teaching on constructive work could be the means of giving a fresh lease of life to non-violent resistance. But that by no means exhausts its value. It has also to be remembered that it provides the best possible evidence of one's good will; and hence, that it has a vital role in connection with the moral appeal which the satyagrahi directs at his opponents. In brief, it goes far in itself to justify Gandhi's own verdict on satyagraha: 'it blesses him who uses it, and him against whom it is used'.

SHORT READING LIST

GANDHI, M. K., *The Story of My Experiments with Truth*, Phoenix Press, 1949.

GANDHI, M. K., *Satyagraha in South Africa*, Nowajivan Publishing House, 1950.

GANDHI, M. K., *Satyagraha (1910–1935)*, Nowajivan Publishing House, 1935.

GANDHI, M. K., *Non-violence in Peace and War*, vols. I and II, Nowajivan Publishing House, 1942 and 1949.

ASHE, GEOFFREY, *Gandhi: a Study in Revolution*, Heinemann, 1968.

BONDURANT, JOAN V., *Conquest of Violence*, Oxford University Press, 1958.

DHAWAN, GOPINATH, *The Political Philosophy of Mahatma Gandhi*, Nowajivan Publishing House, 1951.

DIWAKAR, R. R., *Satyagraha: Its Technique and History*, Hindkitabs, Bombay, 1946.

ERIKSON, ERIK H., *Gandhi's Truth*, Faber and Faber, 1970.

GREGG, RICHARD R., *The Power of Non-violence*, Routledge, 1936.

HORSBURGH, H. J. N., *Non-violence and Aggression*, Oxford University Press, 1968.

NAESS, ARNE, *Gandhi and the Nuclear Age*, Bedminster Press, 1965.

NANDA, B. R., *Mahatma Gandhi*, Allen and Unwin, 1958.

SHRIDHARANI, KRISHNALAL, *War without Violence*, Bharatiya Vidya Bhavan, Bombay, 1962.